Blogging

Table of Contents

Introduction

I want to thank you and congratulate you for purchasing this book...

This book will teach you how to earn money through your blog.

I t will help you become a skilled blogger. It will provide you with tips, tricks, techniques, and strategies that you can use as a blogger. It is a comprehensive guide: it will teach you how to start a blog, write content, promote your site, sell ads, join ad networks, and many more.

It contains screenshots, detailed explanations, and step-by-step instructions. Thus, after reading this book, you will be able to create a blog that generates income. It will also help you enhance your writing and marketing skills. If you want to be a skilled blogger, this is the book that you need to read.

Thanks again for purchasing this book, I hope you enjoy it!

Chapter 1:

How to Establish Your Own Blog

This chapter will teach you how to create your own blog. It will provide you with screenshots and detailed instructions. Thus, you won't experience any problems setting up your blog even if you're not familiar with the process.

1. Search for a Domain – First, you need to find the perfect domain name for your blog. As a general rule, your chosen domain name must be directly linked to the topic/s you will write about. For example, if you're going to write articles about the game of chess, you might consider "chesslessons.com," "letsplaychess.net," or "thechessblog.org."

Since websites can't share a domain name, you need to make sure that your chosen domain is available. Visit www.domize.com and enter the domain name you want to use. The website will help you check the availability of the domain names you selected. It will also give you numerous suggestions, which can be handy if the original domain name you entered is already taken.

2. Purchase the domain name and get a hosting package for your website – Countless hosting service providers are out in the market. Some of the best webhosts are GoDaddy, Network Solutions and Hostgator. To keep this book simple, let's assume that you chose to get the services of Hostgator.

3. Install the WordPress software – After purchasing the domain and hosting package, you must install the WordPress software on your new site. This process can be technical so you are advised to contact your webhost. Basically, you need to contact Hostgator. Once a customer service representative answers your call, inform him/her that you need to install the WordPress program. Then, follow the representative's instructions. Get the login credentials for your WordPress account once the installation process is complete.

4. Access the WordPress system – Launch your favorite web browser and type the following address: www.domainname.com/wp-admin. Just replace the "domainname.com" with your own domain name. Then, enter your login information (i.e. username and password). Once you're logged in, you may start publishing posts and/or customizing your blog.

The Basics of Blogging

This part of the book will explain the basic concepts related to blogging. Read this material carefully since it will help you become an effective blogger.

Blogs

The term "blog" originated from the phrase "web log." In general, blogs are websites that contain viewable materials (e.g. articles). Most "bloggers" (i.e. the people who have blogs) use their blogs as online diaries.

Several years ago, bloggers needed to be familiar with one or more programming languages. Fortunately, blogging platforms (e.g. WordPress) and software producers turned blogging into a simple activity. These days, you can create great blogs even if you don't know any programming language.

Some Thoughts About Starting a Blog

Establishing your own blog is easy and simple. You will surely encounter problems during the first few months of your site. However, you don't have to worry since there are a lot of resources you can use to solve your problems. There are also some online forums that you can join to get answers for your questions.

The Costs

These days, you can start a blog without spending any money. If you want to try how blogging works, it would be best if you will take advantage of the free blog hosting services currently available. This way, you will know whether you really want to be a blogger or not without wasting your funds.

Once you're sure that you want to be a blogger, you should host your own blog. People who want to earn money from their blog/s find more success by getting a hosting package for their site. Self-hosted blogs involve costs, but they are not expensive. In fact, you can get a self-hosted blog for just $15/month.

Chapter 2:

How to Earn Money Through Your Blog

T his chapter will teach you how to monetize your blog. It will provide you with tips, tricks, and techniques that you can use to start earning money from your new site.

The Techniques

CPC (i.e. Cost Per Click) Ads

A lot of bloggers monetize their sites using Cost Per Click ads. As its name suggests, a CPC ad system pays you each time a guest clicks on an ad. Adsense, one of Google's advertising programs, is the most popular CPC option nowadays. With Adsense, Google will check your articles. Then, it will search for advertisements that are related to those articles. Since the ads are related to the actual blog entries, this advertising technique produces excellent results.

Important Note: You will learn more about Adsense later in this chapter.

This system offers a lot of benefits to bloggers and readers. It helps bloggers to earn money from their online articles. Meanwhile, it helps readers find products and/or services that they need.

CPM (i.e. Cost Per Thousand) Ads

This kind of ad system pays you based on the number of visitors who see the ads. The "M" in CPM stands for the Roman numeral that represents 1,000. You won't earn much from this ad system during the first few months of your blogging career. However, once your blog gets a large number of traffic, CPM can help you earn large amounts of money. Here are the most popular CPM networks today:

- Adbrite.com
- Pulsepoint.com
- Casalemedia.com
- AdClickMedia.com
- Technoratimedia.com
- Adify.com

Each of these networks has distinct pros and cons. It would be best if you will analyze each network before getting them on your blog. This way, you can make sure that the CPM network you're using matches your needs.

Affiliate Products

As a blogger, you can act as the intermediary between sellers and potential buyers. You may form partnerships with people or businesses who offer products and/or services that are related to your blog. Then, you will recommend those products/services through your blog posts. In this setup, you will earn money whenever one of your readers pays for the said products/services.

This advertising system turns you into a salesperson. However, unlike traditional salespeople, you can promote products and/or services to countless people and form partnerships with numerous sellers.

Here are some of the best affiliate programs that you can use for your site:

- Flexoffers.com
- LinkShare.com
- Shareasale.com
- CJ.com
- E-Junkie.com
- Affiliate-program.amazon.com
- Panthera.com
- LogicalMedia.com
- RedPlum.com
- MoneySavingMom.com
- Coupons.com
- MySavings.com

It would be best if you will be honest with each of your recommendations. Give objective opinion about the products and/or services you display on your blog. For instance, you may create an article that lists the pros and cons of a product to educate your readers regarding that market offering.

This system works well because it helps three parties simultaneously. You earn money for your referrals. Sellers get more customers. Your readers, on the other hand, learn about the products/services that they might need. You will learn more about affiliate advertising later.

Ad Space

You also have the option to offer ad space to online marketers. Countless bloggers have tried this system and succeeded. Selling ad space to marketers is highly effective when used in niche markets. To apply this ad system on your blog, just visit the www.buysellads.com website. That website helps marketers and bloggers get connected.

The Timeframe

Now that you know how to monetize your blog, you probably want to know how long it would take for you to earn a consistent stream of income. It's important to point out that blogging is not the fastest way to earn money. It involves a long timeframe. Even the best bloggers needed to wait months (or even years) just to get a satisfactory level of income.

Obviously, you can shorten the timeframe significantly if you are already familiar with advertising, content creation, search engine optimization, and other topics related to blogging.

How to Use Adsense Effectively

This part of the book will provide you with advanced techniques. These techniques are designed to boost your earnings from Google's

Adsense program. By applying these techniques on your site, you can double (or even triple) your income from Adsense.

It's important to point out that each blog is unique. Even blogs that belong to the same niche can have different layouts, readers, and articles. These elements greatly influence potential earnings from the Adsense program. However, the techniques given below can help you with your Adsense campaign regardless of your niche, layout, and current blog entries.

1. Place ads on places that attract the readers' eyes – Keep in mind that you earn money from Adsense each time a reader clicks on the displayed ads. That means you need to place those ads in the attractive parts of your blog. However, you also need to consider the overall usability of your site. If you will place Adsense ads with reckless abandon, readers might stop visiting your blog. To gain maximum benefits from Adsense, you need to master the art of ad placement.

2. Target specific parts of your blog entries – With this technique, you will pinpoint the exact parts of your articles that Google must check when choosing ads. Implementing this technique on your blog is simple and easy. You just have to type "<!-- google_ad_section_start →" to indicate the place where Google should start checking. Then, use "<!-- google_ad_section_end → to indicate the endpoint for Google's analysis.

3. Use the plugin called "Quick Adsense" - This plugin, which is offered by the WordPress system, lets you incorporate

Adsense ads into your articles. With this tool, you can choose different criteria to customize the placements of your ads.

Important Note: According to experienced bloggers, the best spot to place an ad is right under the title of a blog entry. You can use Quick Adsense to place ads on that spot.

4. Blend colors – When the Adsense program was introduced, bloggers used loud colors to make ads more interesting. These days, however, bloggers change the colors of Adsense ads so that they blend with the site's theme. The main disadvantage of the old strategy is that it destroys the overall beauty of the blog. The newer strategy resolves this problem by making sure that the blog and the ads are pleasing to the readers' eyes.

5. Create articles for online searchers – You probably have regular readers and visitors from search engine results. In most cases, bloggers don't exert much effort on meeting the needs of visitors who used search engines.

It is true that most of these visitors won't return to your blog again. You need to embrace this fact if you want to succeed as a blogger. Keep in mind that you created a blog to share helpful articles with other people. Thus, you shouldn't worry about the number of times your readers visit your blog.

Search for the keywords used by online searchers. Then, incorporate those keywords to your articles. It doesn't mean that you will ignore your regular readers. Rather, you will write materials that can satisfy the needs of anyone who will visit your blog.

6. Install the search bar of Google – Google is one of the leading search engines today. Its search capabilities are stronger than that of any blogging platform. By installing Google's search bar on your blog, you can help readers find the information they need and earn some money. The results of the online searches come with standard ads, just like typical search results of the Google engine.

7. Connect Adsense and Google Analytics – By linking Adsense and Google Analytics, you can obtain loads of data about your earnings. This technique will help you determine your most profitable articles and best keywords. It can also pinpoint the third-party websites that send the most volume of traffic to your blog. As an Adsense user, you should take advantage of this option.

How to Earn More Money Through Affiliate Advertising

Bloggers consider affiliate advertising as one of the simplest sources of income currently available. It requires you to promote other people's products. With affiliate advertising, you will only earn money if a reader performs a certain action (e.g. buy something, register for an account, download an eBook, etc.).

To earn money through this channel, you must do the following:

1. register for one or more affiliate programs
2. encourage readers to do the action required by the advertiser
3. get paid each time a reader performs the required action

For example, let's say you promoted an eBook that costs $2. Because of the affiliate program, you will get $1 each time one of your readers downloads that eBook. Thus, if 50 people purchase that eBook, you will get $50 as "affiliate income."

In most cases, affiliate programs involve products that must be sold. However, there are also some programs that don't require purchases. For instance, if you are an affiliate of www.coupons.com, you will just post a coupon from that website. You will get paid each time a reader prints that coupon. This kind of program pays up to $0.80 per printed coupon.

Now that you know how affiliate advertising works, it's time to discuss how you can earn loads of money from it.

Here are some tips that can help you maximize your affiliate earnings:

- Consider your values – Affiliate advertising can serve as an excellent source of income. However, it involves potential problems that you should know about. For example, if the product you're promoting has poor quality, your reputation might be ruined. That means you shouldn't promote or write positive reviews about a product just because you can earn money from it. Before crafting any post regarding an affiliate program, ask yourself whether you will write that post even if you won't get anything in return. This way, you can make sure that you will give objective opinions regarding the product you're promoting.

- Use your posts for affiliate ads – You need to incorporate affiliate ads into your blog entries, instead of placing "affiliate links" on your blog's sidebar. Prior to writing a post about a product, find out whether the seller offers an affiliate program. This is an excellent way for you to increase your earnings.

- Try new stuff – Learning how to implement affiliate marketing on your blog requires time and patience. It's possible that you will experience failures during the first few months of your blog. However, don't be discouraged. Try new techniques, change how you promote affiliate links, and identify the methods that work for you.

- Be honest – Give honest opinions about the affiliate products you are promoting. It is also important to inform your readers whenever you promote other people's products. This way, your readers will know that you are getting something each time the promoted product is purchased. Online readers appreciate honesty – countless bloggers have received positive feedback from their readers because of this simple strategy.

- Don't place excessive affiliate links on your site – Don't sign up for each affiliate program you will encounter. It would be best if you will choose affiliate programs that match your blog's "vision" and "mission." Consistency plays a crucial part in the world of blogging. Make your readers feel that your posts and the products you are promoting are related.

Chapter 3:

How to Attract Visitors

Most people create a blog so they can share their thoughts and/or experiences with others. Unfortunately, readers won't visit a blog unless they know that it exists and that it contains useful information. To become a successful blogger, you need to know how to generate traffic for your site.

This chapter will teach you how to attract readers. You need to read this material carefully since it can help you maximize your earnings from your blog.

Comment on Other Blogs

This is one of the best techniques that you can use. Here, you will just place thoughtful responses on other people's blog posts. Great comments can drive a lot of visitors to your site. Bloggers are usually social – being active in the "bloggers' community" can be extremely rewarding. Aside from giving you extra visits, this technique will help you establish relationships with other members of the community.

Post on Other Sites

With this technique, you can get hundreds (or thousands) of readers quickly. Bloggers have used it to boost the traffic of their sites.

This technique requires you to write great articles and submit them to other websites. It's important to note that you should submit unpublished articles only. Other websites won't benefit from materials that have already been published. However, there are websites that allow you to republish your articles (you will learn about this later).

Submitting your work to other sites is easy. You just have to look for blogs that belong to your niche. Comment on the posts inside those blogs and befriend their owners. Finally, tell them that you would like to submit unpublished articles.

Join Blog Networks

You can boost the traffic of your blog by expanding your blogging network. Two of the leading online communities for bloggers are www.blogcatalog.com and www.technorati.com. Join these communities and search for blogs that are related to yours. Building relationships with other bloggers will improve the overall traffic of your site. Additionally, establishing a wide network is one of the best things that you can do as a new blogger.

Join the Blogcarnival.com Website

Expert bloggers recommend this technique to newbies. Basically, www.blogcarnival.com is a website that allows you to share articles you've published before. That means you can use this site to promote the contents of your own blog. Blogcarnival.com can help you get a lot of traffic, especially if your articles have interesting titles.

Join Blog Directories

Inexperienced bloggers need to look for blog directories that are related to their topic. This technique is so important that you must do it before writing blog entries. Here, you will just access your favorite search engine, type your chosen topic, add the word "directory," and hit the Enter key. Your screen will show you blog directories that are relevant to your chosen subject.

As a general rule, you should stay away from directories that offer 100% acceptance. Search for directories that will check your blog before approving it. This technique will help you ensure that you are dealing with topnotch directories. Here are some of the best directories that you can join:

- www.joeant.com
- www.blogged.com
- www.botw.org
- www.greenstalk.com
- www.dmoz.org
- dir.yahoo.com
- www.familyfriendlysites.com

Comment on Message Boards

You can increase the number of visitors to your site by being active in message boards or online forums. Place the URL of your site on your forum account's signature line. Run online searches for forums that are related to your blog.

Here's a basic rule that you should remember: Make sure that all of your posts on the forums are genuine and on-topic. If you will try to promote your site in each of your posts, other bloggers will just get annoyed. They will know what you're trying to do, and your plan will surely backfire.

Create Pages on Other Sites

There are some sites (e.g. www.hubpages.com, www.squidoo.com, www.infobarrel.com, etc.) that let you create a page about any topic. Establishing this kind of site is easy and simple. As an added bonus, this kind of page usually gets excellent search engine rankings.

If this "basic page" acquires lots of traffic, your main blog will also gain more visitors. You can also monetize your "basic page/s", which means you will have more opportunities to earn through your online articles.

Chapter 4:

SEO and Blogging

Y ou might need to wait a long time just to get sufficient traffic from search engines (e.g. Google, Yahoo!, Bing, etc.). In general, search engines are "unfriendly" when it comes to new sites. Search engines prefer established and reputable websites. This is the reason why you need to get associated with legit directories, bloggers, and sites.

Your site will benefit from search engines once it has a lot of links and pages. That means you just have to be patient while expanding your site. Continue writing excellent content – after some time, you will be able to reap the benefits offered by search engines.

In this chapter, you will learn about the different SEO techniques that are compatible with blogs. Read this chapter carefully since it will aid you in boosting your blog's overall traffic.

SEO – The Basics

SEO (Search Engine Optimization) helps websites in getting excellent rankings in the search engine results. Your website will get a lot of free traffic if it can obtain great rankings for related keywords. This book won't give detailed explanations of all the SEO techniques currently available.

Rather, it will focus on the basic techniques that inexperienced bloggers can use. Keep in mind that you don't need to be an SEO expert to earn money from your blog. You just have to understand how SEO works and how you can use it for your site.

Search engines are designed to help searchers find the content, products, and/or services that they need. These "engines" want to show websites that are relevant to the searchers' needs. The system used by these engines aren't perfect. However, Google and other search engines are continuously working to improve the accuracy of their results.

Important Note: Never try to trick search engines. Your site will get punished once these engines catch you. Rather than finding and exploiting the technical issues of search engines, you should focus on writing content that can educate and/or entertain your readers.

The SEO Techniques

This part of the book will arm you with fundamental SEO techniques. If you will use these techniques properly, your site will get excellent rankings in the search results pages.

- Use Proper Title Tags – Bloggers consider this as one of the most important SEO techniques.
  Basically, title tags are the words/phrases/sentences that appear at the top section of a browser. Search engines consider the title tags of a website while determining its rank.

- Include keywords in the title tags of your webpages. In addition, you need to make sure that your title tags are related to your content. For instance, if you wrote an article about chess, you don't want to use "Best Basketball Drills" as the title tag for that particular entry.

- Incorporate Keywords to Your Anchor Texts – An "anchor text" is the word or phrase you will use when creating a link. For example, if you will place your mouse pointer over this link, you will see that it points to the Yahoo! website. In this example, "this link" serves as the anchor text. This element of content creation is important because it gives a lot of information about your site.

- Search engines consider anchor texts when ranking websites. As you know, it's not possible to manipulate how other bloggers create anchor texts when linking to your website. However, you should incorporate relevant keywords to your anchor texts whenever you can. For example, you may use keyword-rich anchor texts when linking to the posts and pages within your blog. You may also use this technique on your directory submissions and forum signature lines.

- Choose Keywords Carefully – If you want to earn money through your blog, you should identify what potential readers are searching for. You can maximize the benefits of this technique if you will do it before writing any article. There are numerous keyword tools available online. Use these tools to find the hottest keywords that are related to your chosen topic.

- Get Inbound Links – Inbound links play an important role in any SEO campaign. Acquiring links that point to your site is one of the most effective techniques for improving a website's search engine rankings. As a bonus, inbound links can send potential readers straight to your blog. Many bloggers overlook this fact. Your blog will enjoy a spike in overall traffic if popular blogs or sites point to it.

The Tools

In this part of the book, you will discover the tools that can boost your site's traffic and search engine rankings.

- www.bigstock.com - This is one of the best websites that offer stock photography. With www.bigstock.com, you can get great images without spending much money. In general, articles become more attractive and pleasing to the eye when they contain images. Thus, if you want your readers to enjoy your written work, you should add pictures to them.
- www.google.com/webmasters/tools – This tool shows you how Google sees your blog. It will also pinpoint the problems that are affecting your blog's rankings in the search results pages.
- www.google.com/analytics – This powerful tool helps you in tracking and analyzing your readers. Google has integrated this tool with Adsense. Thus, it can now provide you with more useful information.
- www.mailchimp.com – Email marketing can help you attract more visitors. If you just want to try email marketing, www.mailchimp.com is the best tool for you. With this tool,

you can get up to 2,000 email subscribers without shelling out any money.

- tools.seobook.com/keyword-tools – You can use this tool to determine how many online searchers use certain keywords. Keywords play a crucial part in your blog's SEO campaign so you should add this tool to your arsenal.

Chapter 5:

Writing Content

You won't earn money from your blog if you can't write great content. That's because you need sufficient traffic in order to earn income from your website. As you probably know, nothing beats great content when it comes to attracting website traffic.

If you will ask experienced bloggers for advice on how to succeed, almost all of them will tell you to write excellent content for your site.

In this chapter, you will learn the basics of high-quality content. It will also provide you with tips and techniques that can help you write effective blog posts.

Write Articles that are Unique, Engaging, and Valuable

To become successful, you need to write unique content. If your blog has unique articles, readers will keep on visiting it. If you will just rewrite published materials, on the other hand, people won't visit your website. They'll prefer to read the original material.

Next, write articles that are engaging. The main reason why blogs gained immense popularity is the fact that they allow readers to interact with the writers. Thus, as a blogger, you won't be having any monologue (unless no one reads and reacts to your materials).

People will visit your site, read the stuff you wrote, and react through comments or emails. That means you will interact with your readers actively. In order to create a well-known site, you must establish an online community for it. Here are the things you can do to establish a great community for your blog:

- Be personal, especially when writing your materials
- Ask your readers directly
- Write comments based on your readers' previous comments
- Share your ideas and opinions only during appropriate situations

Lastly, your content should be valuable. If the materials you will publish don't have any value, no one will visit your blog. The value of your materials may differ, based on the topic you're writing about. For instance, if your blog focuses on tech news, you need to craft blog entries that inform your readers about the latest technological developments. If your blog focuses on humor, however, you must create posts that make your readers laugh.

Write Killer Articles

Basically, killer articles are blog entries that contain exceptional value for the readers. Whenever a reader encounters a killer article, he/she will blog and/or Tweet about it, bookmark it, and inform other people about the article's existence.

Often, a killer article is structured and contains a lot of words. However, you're not required to use thousands of words in order to create killer articles. Let's assume that you have a chess blog and that you discovered a new strategy to destroy White in the Ruy Lopez opening. This kind of topic will surely produce a "killer," even if you will keep the article concise. That's because the article offers enormous value for your readers (considering that the Ruy Lopez is one of the most popular openings today).

As a blogger, you should consider killer articles as the foundation of your content development scheme. This way, you can generate website traffic, attract inbound links, and present yourself as an authority in your chosen niche. Killer articles may take any of these formats:

- Rankings (e.g. Top 10 Chess Players of the 21st Century)
- Lists (e.g. The 5 Opening Blunders You Must Avoid)
- Breaking News (e.g. Magnus Carlsen Defends His Crown for the 20th Time)
- Resources (e.g. Free Chess eBooks You Can Download Today)
- Elaborated Interviews (e.g. Ten Chess Opening Experts: The Downfall of the Semi-Slav Opening)
- In-depth Analysis (e.g. Your Detailed Guide to the Caro-Kann Opening)

Killer articles require you to perform researches and analyses. In addition, these kinds of article are more complex than ordinary ones. Fortunately, the results you can get from killer articles are definitely worth it.

Lastly, publish killer articles on a regular basis. It would be great if you can publish a killer article each week. If your schedule doesn't permit that, however, try to create a killer article once per month.

Regular Posts

It is true that killer articles will attract new readers and establish your authority in the niche you are in. However, you can't rely on killer articles all the time. You also need to write regular blog entries to create an online community for your site. Regular posts let you interact directly with your readers.

In addition, ordinary posts can help you ensure the smooth flow of your blog's contents. Creating killer articles on a daily basis would require lots of effort. Achieving this unlikely goal wouldn't benefit your blog in anyway – it will just overload your audience with complex and disconnected bits of information. Here are the most popular variants of ordinary posts:

- Polls (e.g. Who is Your Favorite Chess Player?)
- Events (e.g. Chess World Championship 2016)
- Site Updates (e.g. The Latest Features of www.thechessblog.com)
- Quick Links (e.g. 10 Tips for Sicilian Defense Fanatics)
- Opinion Pieces (e.g. Garry Kasparov's Greatest Strengths)

Headlines

You need to know the importance of headlines if you want to be a successful blogger. Keep in mind that you need to find the best headline for each of your blog posts. Actually, some experienced bloggers suggest that the amount of time you will spend on finding a headline should be equal to the time you spent on writing the article itself.

The headline is important because it attracts your readers. There are countless blog entries on the internet today – readers choose the ones they want to read based on the articles' headlines. Readers look at the headline of your article before reading its content. If your headline sucks, readers might ignore your article completely.

Headlines affect your current and potential readers. For example, if your post has a bad headline, even your regular readers will skip it. The time available to online readers is severely limited. They won't waste their time on materials that are "probably useless." Additionally, if you will submit that article to social bookmarking websites (e.g. www.digg.com), readers won't click on it.

Effective headlines have two main elements, which are:

1. Wording – The headline's wording should match your readers' mindset. This element informs potential readers that the article they're looking at contains the information they need. Here, knowledge regarding keyword selection can help you greatly.

You may use Google's "Keyword Tool" for this. Basically, "Keyword Tool" is a service that generates 150 words related to the keyword you will enter. This tool will also display the search volume of each related term. For example, if you will launch the Keyword Tool and type "energy," your screen will show you this:

Write Down Your Ideas

Bloggers usually have problems in generating new ideas. You can solve this problem by writing down your thoughts. Write down all of your ideas that may lead to blog entries. You may use any tool for this process (e.g. a notebook, a text editor, a whiteboard, etc.). It doesn't matter what tool you use. If your tool lets you store, organize, and retrieve your ideas, you're good to go.

As an alternative, you may create a draft whenever you get an interesting idea. Just launch your preferred blogging program and record your thoughts. Type down the entry's title and main points. You don't have to finish the article in one sitting. Save the entry as a draft (if you can't complete it now) and work on it again once you have the time for it.

If the strategies given above are not enough to generate a consistent stream of ideas, you may launch Google's Keyword Tool and enter some keywords that are relevant to your topic. Find the long versions of the keywords and use them as the basis for your future articles.

Lastly, you may visit social bookmarking websites. This strategy will help you discover the hottest topics on the internet. Here are the leading bookmarking sites today:

- www.delicious.com
- www.digg.com
- www.reddit.com
- www.stumbleupon.com

The Frequency of Your Posts

There is no such as thing as "ideal frequency" for publishing blog entries. Some blogs get updated once per week.

Other blogs, however, display several new posts on a daily basis.

It is important to point out that quality is more important than quantity. Thus, you need to make sure that all of your posts are useful for your readers and your website. Refraining from posting new articles is better than posting bad materials. The absence of new posts requires your readers to wait. The presence of low-quality posts, on the other hand, can ruin the image and popularity of your blog.

To earn money from your blog, you should strike a balance with quantity and quality. This is the reason why most of the greatest blogs today publish new entries daily. If your schedule doesn't let you post every day, try to be consistent regarding the time you publish blog entries. For instance, you can publish three new posts each week and follow that schedule.

To maximize the benefits you can get from being consistent, try to publish new content on the same day/s each week. This way, you can assure your readers that they will find new entries on your site.

Five Tips for Crafting Excellent Posts

1. Be true to yourself – Inexperienced bloggers tend to imitate the writing style of other people. They do this in order to display a false air of confidence and/or authority. Unfortunately, this tendency can lead to complex problems in the future. Rather than trying to imitate other blogger's style, you should try to find your own "writing voice" and improve it.

You have unique characteristics. Your skills and abilities are different from those of other bloggers. You view things differently, because you are different from others.

Study the techniques used by other bloggers. This approach allows you to enhance your writing skills quickly and easily. However, keep in mind that you are different from them.

2. Show that you are confident – New bloggers often get discouraged whenever they see other blogs that have a lot of traffic, updates, creative posts, social media followers, or comments. These

inexperienced bloggers worry too much about failing to emulate the achievements of their "seniors."

You won't benefit from worrying or sulking in a corner. If you're not happy with your current skills, do what you can to improve them. Try to show your confidence in your blog posts. Posts that were confidently written have high chances of turning visitors to regular readers.

3. Engage your readers – Communicate with your audience. Reply to their emails and comments when you have the time. Take note of your readers' input and advice. Make your readers feel that you value them. This way, you can strengthen the loyalty of your readers.

Spice things up by publishing off-topic photos, videos or posts. These "surprising" blog entries can keep your blog exciting. Additionally, you must try new blogging techniques. Writing posts using the same technique over and over again can result to bored readers and poor website traffic.

4. Be honest – You don't need to be perfect in order to write great stuff. In blogging, honesty is more important than apparent perfection. Don't give the impression that you know everything and that all of your actions are correct.

You can attract a lot of readers just by being open and honest. In some cases, you also need to show your weaknesses.

5. Review and edit your output thoroughly – Readers don't like typos and grammar mistakes. If you want to earn money through your blog, you need to enhance your writing and proofreading skills.

Sloppy writing can ruin your plans. You can secure the quality of your blog by proofreading each post twice prior to publishing it. Work on your writing skills constantly. Read excellent blogs and books. Be objective while reviewing your work.

Here are some tips that can help you write great content:

- Don't write huge paragraphs – Online readers get turned off by huge paragraphs. As you probably know, reading large blocks of characters on a monitor is not fun. You can enhance the readability of your posts by reducing the size of your paragraphs.

- Be consistent regarding the font you're using.

- Don't use ellipses, all caps, or exclamation points unnecessarily.

- If your post contains multiple paragraphs, use subheadings.

- Add photos and/or videos to your posts.

Chapter 6:

Site Design and Functionality

This chapter will teach you how to improve your site's design and functionality aspects. Study this material carefully: your site's look and usability greatly affect the income you can earn from your written works.

The Free Stuff

Inexperienced bloggers must not spend a large amount of money on their blog's design. Most blogging platforms offer beautiful themes for free. For example, WordPress has various themes you can choose from. You just have to log in to your WordPress account and access the page called Themes Directory.

Additionally, there are blogs and websites that offer lists of excellent themes. Launch your favorite web browser, type the right keywords (e.g. "best themes wordpress"), and hit the Enter key. In just a few seconds, your screen will show you list of the best themes currently available.

You can easily customize the free themes offered by WordPress. Thus, you can personalize your blog completely even without spending any money.

You can also benefit from studying basic CSS and HTML. These topics can help you improve the look of your blog. Currently, there are countless eBooks and online articles written about CSS and HTML. You will get all the resources you need just by running an online search.

Your Blog's Logo

If you have some money for your blog's design, use it to get a logo. That's because you can use the logo of your blog on any theme, design, or template. It will also strengthen your brand and improve the uniqueness of your blog.

Currently, www.99designs.com is the leading website when it comes to purchasing logos. With this site, you can

obtain an excellent logo   for just $150.

Implement Prioritization

Your readers can do a wide range of things while on your blog. Here are some examples:

- read one post
- read a lot of posts
- read the "most viewed" posts
- subscribe to your site's RSS feed
- click on an ad

- purchase products through the affiliate links on your blog
- sign up for your email newsletter
- add a comment
- download an eBook
- buy a product you're selling
- share one or more posts with others

However, there is no blog design that can encourage all of the activities listed above. Many bloggers have tried, but without success. These bloggers succeeded in filling their sites with clutter, confusing their readers, and reducing their blog's effectiveness.

That means you must prioritize certain user activities over others. It would be best if you will list down the five user activities that are important for your blog. Then, design your blog so that it emphasizes the activities you listed down. If a design element doesn't match your priorities, you should either remove it or transfer it to a different part of the website.

Encourage Subscriptions

The previous section required you to list down the most important activities for your site. Well, encouraging email and RSS subscribers should be at the top of your list. That's because registered subscribers often become regular readers. In addition, you can easily establish relationships with readers who view your content on a regular basis.

Most bloggers support user subscriptions through RSS feeds. This option is good, but you shouldn't rely on it exclusively. To improve your chances of succeeding, offer email subscriptions too. If you have a Twitter account, you may also ask your readers to follow you on that social networking site so they can get updates easily.

Your "Bestseller"

While designing your blog, you should also strive to display your best posts. This way, new visitors can easily find the best articles your blog has to offer. By showing excellent contents to your first time readers, you will have better chances of converting them into regular visitors. They might also sign up for your email and/or RSS feed subscription offers.

You can display your best materials in two ways. First, you can create a "best material" area within your blog. Most bloggers choose the header, footer, or the sidebar for this purpose.
To list your best articles, you may use HTML codes to add the links manually. If you want to automate this task, on the other hand, you may use a plugin offered by your blogging platform.

For the second option, you will create a webpage inside your blog to showcase your best content. Here, you may divide your posts based on their category or date of original publication. After creating the webpage, you may display its link on your blog's sidebar or main menu. You may boost the appearance of your blog by replacing the link with a relevant image.

The Mistakes Related to Usability

This part of the book will discuss the most common usability mistakes committed by inexperienced bloggers. Read this material carefully – it will help you provide excellent user experience to your site visitors.

- Old records are hard to find – Your blog should have a page that contains all of your previous posts. Adding an archives section to your blog helps your readers in finding the material they need. It can also enhance your rankings in the search engine results pages.
- Search boxes aren't available – People use search boxes in order to find the information they need. Some individuals even use a search box to reach different parts of a website. Your users might get frustrated if your blog doesn't have any search box.
- The site's structure is too complex – As a blogger, you need to keep your site's structure simple. Here are some things that you can do to improve the structure of your blog: (1) eliminating/minimizing drop-down options, (2) adding a navigation bar, and (3) making sure that all of your blog's webpages have a link that points to its homepage.
- Poor typography – Your readers will stop visiting your blog if they have problems reading your content. Use the proper font size for your blog entries. Ensure that the spacing between lines and letters are enough. Lastly, make sure that your webpages contain sufficient amounts of "white space."

- Excessive advertisements – Some bloggers think that they need to place numerous ads on their site just to make money. Well, nothing could be further from the truth. You will only make money from blogging if you have great website traffic. Unfortunately, readers don't like excessive ads. That means placing lots of ads on your blog can actually diminish your site's traffic and your overall income.

  It would be best if you will start with a few advertisements. Increase the number of ads slowly. Make sure that this "monetizing" process doesn't affect the user experience received by your readers.

- Problematic links – Links play an important role in your site's navigation. In general, your readers should be able to recognize links easily. That means you should underline the hyperlinks inside your posts. If you're not fond of extra lines, however, you may change the color of the hyperlinks. This way, your readers can easily identify the clickable and non-clickable parts of your blog entries.

- Too much widgets, badges and buttons – Inexperienced bloggers usually commit this mistake. Adding a badge, a widget, or a button is easy and simple. As a result, bloggers use these tools to decorate their sidebars.

  The habit of installing unnecessary items on a webpage can hurt your site's traffic. Excessive buttons, widgets, and/or badges don't contribute in increasing your content's value. Rather, they can actually confuse and/or frustrate your readers.

Chapter 7:

The Networking Aspects of Blogging

T hese days, the people/organizations you are linked to have the same value as the things you actually do. That statement also applies to blogging.

If you can build great relationships with other bloggers, you will obtain a lot of backlinks. Additionally, these people will recommend your site to their readers and assist you in selling products and/or services. Simply put, networking can help you earn money.

This chapter will teach you how to conduct proper networking. It will provide you with tips and strategies to help you build an effective network.

Real Connections

When it comes to networking, you should always focus on establishing "real" connections with other people. Don't approach a blogger just because he/she is rich, important, or popular. Rather, establish relationships with the bloggers who have earned your respect. Find people whose materials you can gladly recommend to your own readers.

If you will follow the tip given above, you will be able to form win-win relationships with the people who can help you best. Keep in mind that networking involves the principle of mutualism: help others if you want them to help you. Be ready to support the bloggers who belong to your network.

List Blogs Down

Before establishing your online network, list down the blogs that belong to your chosen niche.

you may also include blogs that belong to niches that are related to yours.

If you want,

The number of blogs you have to list down depends on the niche you are in. If you are working on a tech blog, your list should contain about 200 items. If you're blogging about cockatoos, however, 10 to 15 blogs must be enough. While doing this task, you need to get all of the information available to you. This list will help you build your network. If your list is incomplete, your chances of succeeding will be extremely low.

To find blogs that belong to particular niches, use the following tools:

- www.alltop.com
- www.blogcatalog.com
- www.technorati.com

- www.blogrank.com
- www.wikio.com/blogs/top

Approach the Bloggers

After creating your list, you need to approach the owners of the blogs you found. Almost all blogs have an email address or contact form. Visit the blogs one by one and check their "Contact Us" page (if applicable).

The following tips will help you in introducing yourself:

- Be straight to the point. Say what you want to say.
- Tell them that you are blogging about the same niche/topic/industry. Include your blog's URL in your signature line or in the content of your message.
- If the content of their blog interests you, inform them. Additionally, tell them that you would like to link to their published materials if it's okay.

Link to Other Sites When Appropriate

You should link to other sites in order to get links for your own blog. Obviously, other bloggers will likely create links that go to your site if you will do the same for them first. As you can see, the "golden rule" also applies to online networking.

It would be great if you will subscribe to the RSS feeds of the blogs you listed. With this trick, you will keep yourself updated regarding the hottest trends in your chosen topic. In addition, it will help you find great articles from the blogs you have subscribed to. Whenever you find an awesome article, write your own blog entry based on it, say whatever you want to say regarding the topic, and indicate the URL of the original material.

You may also contact that blogger through an email. Tell him/her that you like his/her work and that you shared it with others.

Lastly, make sure that you are linking to high-quality posts that are related to your niche. Great articles won't help you if there's no connection between them and your blog. Thus, if you're blogging about chess, linking to a post about the newest BMW cars isn't a good idea.

Support the Members of Your Network

Aside from creating outbound links, you can support the people inside your network in many ways. Here are some examples:

- recommend their sites to your friends and readers
- promote their products and/or services
- recommend them for awards or interviews
- share and vote for their blog entries on bookmarking websites
- share their content on social media platforms such as Facebook and Twitter

Important Point: Other bloggers will consider you as a friend if you will continue "giving" without asking for anything in return.

Promote Your Best Posts

The tips and strategies given above focus on doing things for other people. You're probably thinking how you can reap the benefits of having an online network. Well, if you will follow the lessons previously discussed, other bloggers will notice you and promote your blog in return.

This process might take a long time. Fortunately, there's a technique that you can use to encourage other bloggers to link back to your site. This technique requires you to share your blog's "bestsellers" to the bloggers you are trying to attract.

For example, after publishing a killer article, you may send the URL of that article to your target bloggers. While using this technique, you should never beg for backlinks. Just inform the other bloggers that you wrote an article that they might like. Then, provide a link that points to that article.

This approach doesn't pressure the recipients. Thus, they have higher chances of reading, reviewing, and recommending the post you shared. Keep in mind that other bloggers might not give you the backlink you're waiting for. In this situation, stay calm and concentrate on what you need to do. If you will keep on improving your blog and your writing skills, those people will surely link to your posts.

Chapter 8:

How to Earn More Money

This chapter will help you increase your earnings. It will give you tips and techniques that you can use to earn more from your blog.

Monetizing Your Sidebar

Offering sidebar advertisements require a lot of time and effort. However, as numerous bloggers have discovered, sidebar ads can boost blog earnings significantly. In addition, you can implement this scheme regardless of the niche you belong to. By offering sidebar advertisements on your own, you will get full control over the ads that will appear on your blog.

Here are the things that you can do to monetize your sidebar:

- Inform Others – Let other people know that you are offering sidebar ads. Many bloggers wonder why no one buys the sidebar advertisements they are offering. Well, the main reason is that these bloggers don't market their offerings actively. Online marketers won't pay for your sidebar ads if you won't inform them about your offering.

Marketers are usually busy – they won't analyze blogs and see whether the owners offer sidebar ads. Actually, some marketers won't know that you are selling sidebar advertisements unless you indicate it clearly.

Create an advertising page. Then, access your header and add a tab that points to the advertising page you created. Basically, your advertising page must show the following details:

- the demographics of your readers

- testimonials from current and/or previous marketers
- the daily and/or monthly traffic of your blog
- advertising options and prices

Your blog's advertising page must also state why advertisers should choose your site. Let potential advertisers know what they are going to get from your sidebar ads.

- Offer Discounts – If it's your first time selling sidebar advertisements, you may offer discounts to attract potential customers. Create a blog entry that highlights the reduced pricing. Then, forward that post to the companies who might be interested in your sidebar ads.

- Create "Ad Bundles" - Offering basic sidebar ads can generate income. However, you can boost your earnings further by creating "ad bundles." For example, rather than offering a sidebar advertisement for $25/month, offer a two-month "bundle" that contains one sidebar ad, one post about the customer's business, and one link on your email and/or RSS feed for just $70.

Alternatively, you may offer price reductions to people who buy ads that last for several months. This kind of discount leads to a win-win situation for you and your customers. They will be able to reduce their marketing costs, while you won't have to worry about finding new advertisers each month.

- Fill Your Ad Spots – According to experienced bloggers, you shouldn't leave your sidebar ads empty. Don't place an "Advertise Here" sign on your blog. This kind of notice tells potential advertisers that no one wants to pay for your sidebar ads. Obviously, you don't want your potential customers to think that way.

  If there's a free space in your ad spots, use it to promote affiliate products. Alternatively, you may offer free advertising to your friends.

The Pricing

The price that you will charge for your sidebar ads depends on various factors. These factors are:

- the traffic of your blog
- the niche you belong to

- the placement of the ad
- the number of ad spots you're offering
- the current demand for ad spots

Beginners should start with low prices. Increase the amount as you gain more blogging experience and site traffic.

Usually, you will get paid per thousand views. That means you should start with $1 or below per thousand views. If you are currently getting 15,000 views each month, you may get about $15/month for a 250x250 ad that is placed on your sidebar.

Important Note: Don't sell more than eight sidebar advertisements. The overall value of your ads will decrease if you will place a lot of sidebar ads on your blog. In general, few high-paying ads are better than numerous yet cheap ones.

Chapter 9:

Ad Networks

A d networks can serve as a great source of income for bloggers. Basically, an ad network is an advertising broker. You will reserve ad spots on your site and the brokers will sell the spots on your behalf. These brokers will get a fee (30-50% of the total price) each time they successfully sell an ad spot.

Many bloggers love ad networks. On the other hand, there are some bloggers who had horrible experiences because of this kind of network. In this chapter, you will learn the advantages and disadvantages of joining ad networks.

The Advantages

- Ad Networks Can Simplify Complex Tasks – Selling advertising space personally requires a lot of time and effort. By joining an ad network, you can simplify your tasks greatly. With this kind of network, you will just sign the contract, insert HTML codes into your sidebar, and collect the payments.
- Ad Networks Can Help You Earn More – The income that you will earn through an ad network varies widely. Some bloggers earn $1 to $2 per thousand views while others get $20 for the same number of views.

However, ad networks are still better than selling sidebar ads personally. The latter generates $1 (or below) per thousand views. Well, this amount is unacceptable for people who belong to an ad network. On average, network members get $2 to $4 per thousand views. That means joining an advertising network is better than offering ads personally, especially if you're an inexperienced blogger.

- Ad Networks Can Give You Extra Projects – Although the income from ad spots can be great, the income from side projects is often greater. Today, ad networks can provide you with extra projects such as sponsored posts.

Ad networks serve as the middlemen between bloggers and advertisers. Thus, they can give you excellent opportunities you won't find on your own.

The Disadvantages

- Ad Networks Control Your Deals – If you are a member of an ad network, you won't be able to choose which ads will appear on your blog. Most ad networks are not willing to make bloggers decide regarding the ads that will be displayed. This can be a problem – conflicts between your content and the ads you are showing might arise.

- Joining an Ad Network Is Not Easy – Joining an advertising network can take several months. Ad networks, particularly the best ones, have few openings and long waiting lists.

Chapter 10:

Additional Options

The previous chapters taught you how to earn money straight from your blogging activities. However, it is important to note that blogging allows you to earn income indirectly.

In this chapter, you will discover several strategies that you can use to earn extra income. These strategies use your blog indirectly.

- Conduct Online Classes – This strategy can help you learn new things while earning more money.

  Online teaching doesn't require a large capital. In fact, you just have to acquire basic tools (e.g. microphone). Countless bloggers have succeeded in implementing this strategy on their sites.

- Write eBooks – You can also earn money by creating and selling your own eBooks. This option is usually not included in a blogger's arsenal. Well, that's unfortunate. You can earn hundreds (or even thousands) of dollars annually just by writing and selling eBooks.

Writing eBooks can serve as your main source of income, especially during the first few months of your blog. Here are the things you need to keep in mind while using this strategy:

- Write about topics that are practical and relevant. Thus, you need to craft an eBook that teaches people how to do stuff. For example, you may write an eBook that explains how people can lose weight, start a business, become more organized, etc.

- Make sure that your eBook's cover looks amazing.

- Promote your eBooks through different marketing channels.

- Be a Freelancer – Some of your readers might offer you freelancing jobs. This strategy can be extremely profitable, especially if you have excellent writing skills. If you want to get more freelance writing opportunities, you may contact parenting magazines in your country. Most of them pay about $25 for each article.

- Be a Consultant – These days, some companies are hiring bloggers as consultants. Bloggers know a lot about online and social media marketing. Thus, companies are now trying to leverage bloggers' knowledge and experience.

Consulting services can get you about $50/hour. Unfortunately, finding clients can be difficult. Bloggers attract clients through their online networks.

Conclusion

Congratulations for finishing this book!

I hope it will help you earn income through your blog. By reading this book carefully and applying the lessons it contains, you will get regular readers and consistent streams of income.

The next step is to continue improving your writing and marketing skills. Write excellent content and share your materials with others. This way, you can become a blogger who helps his/her readers and gets paid for what he/she is doing.

Finally, if you enjoyed this book, please take the time to share your thoughts and post a positive review on Amazon. It'd be greatly appreciated!

Thank you and good luck!